It's Me, That's Who!

Mark J. Beasley

Illustrations by
Kem Welch

ISBN: 979-8-9910778-0-4

Illustrated by Kem Welch
Produced by Publish Pros | www.publishpros.com

Contents

Acknowledgments

Recognizing those who helped put this project together would take more pages than space will allow. So, to save a few trees, I've narrowed it down:

Kem Welch: whose impressive artwork makes turning pages worth it.

Barbara Welch: whose editing keeps the grammar in order.

John Seymour: whose setup, design, layout, arrangement, placement of drawings, and verses, went far beyond what he signed up for. I am indebted indeed.

Also, all the family and friends I've put on the spot by asking them to read this verse or that line so many times and giving their honest opinion.

I appreciate all of you,
Mark

Inspiration

For the most part, if not the whole part, I'm inspired by writers of clever verse.

The main characters who encompass the spectrum of my focus are:

Shel Silverstein: Where the Sidewalk Ends, *A Light in the Attic, Falling Up*

Jack Prelutsky: *The New Kid on the Block, Hard-Boiled Bugs for Breakfast*

Darren Sardelli: *What If, Galaxy Pizza and Meteor Pie*, children's book author, poet, and speaker at Laugh a Lot Poetry.

For inspiration going back even longer, I'm obligated to thank Theodore Seuss Geisel.

Dr. Seuss

His writing amazes
The words and the phrases
A genius with language was he
When spoken or sung
It rolls off the tongue
As easy as one two three

The reader engages
While turning the pages
Astonished at what is uncovered
Verse beyond measure
Like finding a treasure
Astounded at what is discovered

We can only admire
While we try and aspire
To match his impeccable skill
We can't reproduce
Like the great Dr. Seuss
And nobody ever will.

~ Mark J. Beasley

From there to here,
From here to there,
Funny things are everywhere

~ Theodore Seuss Geisel

It's Me, That's Who

Who am I? It's me, that's who
Who am I? It's me, not you
I'm satisfied down deep inside
And quite delighted too

I like that who I am is me
I like that fact a lot
For it's silly of me
To pretend to be
Someone that I'm not

Who am I? It's me, that's who
Who am I? It's me, not you
I'll always be
Not you, but me
And nobody else will do!

Flashlight

I bought a flashlight yesterday
That doesn't work, therefore
I insist I get my money back
I returned it to the store

It didn't function like a flashlight should
It's as worthless as the trash
Sure, it lit my way in the dark
But I never saw it flash

A Pile of Rope

Penny pulls a pile of rope
Everywhere she goes
'Cause pulling rope is easy
As everybody knows

Since pushing rope is hopeless
Penny simply chose
To pull along a pile of rope
Everywhere she goes

Timbuktu

It's a long, long way
To get to Timbuktu
Three weeks travel
In the fastest canoe

You can march across the desert
But it's tough to get through
Your chances are slim
And survivors are few

You can journey through the jungle
In the thick bamboo
Some never make it
But then, some do

Most give up
Since they really can't take it
But some push forward
As far as they can make it

And anyone will tell you
That's ever gotten through
It's a long, long way
To get to Timbuktu

Farmer Flynn

Farmer Flynn
Built a pen
To keep his cows
And horses in

He built it fast
He built it strong
It's built to last
But something's wrong

It's got no gate
At all, so then
How will he get
The animals in?

Decisions, Decisions

You make decisions
Left up to you
So you have to choose
Between one of the two

Is it this one or that one?
There isn't another
Or that one or this one?
Pick one or the other

One less than two
For two is too many
One is much better
Than not having any

One of the two
No more than one
One or the other
One more than none

You can't have a pair
So pick only one
I know it's not fair
But that's how it's done

Now you have to choose
Between one of the two
So make a decision
It's all up to you

If I Hadn't Been an Eskimo

While walking through

The heavy snow

My body was cold

From head to toe

And I would've froze

To death, I know

If I hadn't been an Eskimo

The Tooth Fairy

"I've lost my tooth"
My sister said
"It fell out the front
Of the back of my head"

"It popped out yesterday
And it's quite confusing
Since this is a tooth
That I was still using"

I told her to place it
Under the pillow tonight
And the fairy would come
When she turned out the light

She believed her tooth
Would be fixed by the fairy
She thought one thing
But quite the contrary

Because she found under her pillow
When she woke from the bed
No tooth like she thought
But money instead

Believing Is Free

There are those who believe
Whatever they see
Whatever it is
Whatever it be

There are those who believe
Whatever they hear
Makes sense to them
It's ever so clear

There are those who believe
Whatever they say
Whatever they preach
Whatever they pray

There are those who believe
Whatever they shouldn't
Who sometimes do
But normally wouldn't

And those who believe
Whatever they will
Who believed in it then
And believe in it still

There are those who believe
Whatever they feel
Whatever they will
Whatever the deal

Whenever the time
Whenever they can
Whenever it fits
Whatever the plan

Whatever it is
Whatever it be
Believe what you want
Believing is free

When Music Fills the Air

The day becomes complete
When music fills the air
It makes the scene enjoyable
Whenever music's there

It brings about an atmosphere
Quite relaxing for so many
It stifles animosity
If ever there was any

It makes the day acceptable
If the day you had was not
Sometimes it helps a little
Sometimes it helps a lot

It neutralizes hectic mornings
It suppresses aches and pains
It frees the average person
From overbearing strains

It eases all your troubles
All your tantrums, all your fits
It makes the day acceptable
However bad it gets

For the day can be unbearable
If no music lingers there
It makes the scene enjoyable
When music fills the air

Now fill the air with music
From some musical device
Any number is sufficient
Any medley will suffice

New Rules

Baseball has new rules this year
The old-fashioned game obsolete
The owners say
The brand-new way
Is more befitting to compete

The pitcher throws a ball of fire
From a mound that's covered with ants
The batter bats with electric wire
And gasoline soaking his pants

Baseball caps are lined with brambles
Their gloves submerged in glue
Cleats are smeared with axle grease
And socks are dipped in goo

The outfield littered with landmines
The infield enveloped in smoke
Scorpions nest on all the bases
Which are covered in poison oak

Between each base lies a booby trap
And strands of razor wire
As they tag each base
The runners all face
Constant machine gun fire

Tarantulas creep in the locker room
That's filled with thousands of roaches
There's an obstacle course in center field
And mosquitoes menace the coaches

Alligators lurk in the dugout
Vampire bats in the air
Piranha swim in the drinking water
And leaches are everywhere

Baseball has new rules this year
It's totally redesigned
Plenty of fans show up to cheer
But players are hard to find

Piles of Pills

Molly Mills
Takes piles of pills
To ease her many
Pains and ills

From muscle cramps
To achy knees
Her runny nose
And nagging sneeze

From headaches
To her tender back
Her aging joints
Are out of whack
Twisted fingers
Tangled toes
A dizzy spell
That comes and goes

Pills for circulation
Pills for evening chills
Pills for relaxation
Poor old Molly Mills

She's ninety-three
And you can see
She's not as young
As she used to be

She's taken countless
Sickness pills
To ease her numerous
Belly ills

For every pain
She pops a pill
She always has
And always will

Guts

A crazy little bug
Slammed into my windshield
And the impact blew out
What used to be in

That crazy little bug
Was certainly courageous
Bet he hasn't got the guts
To try that again

A Tasty Dish

The chef prepared
A tasty dish
And insisted I eat
All I wish

But the plate was bare
No food was there
Not one bite
For me anywhere

When he insisted I eat
All I wish
I guess he meant
To eat the dish

The Thunder Boomed

The clouds loomed
The thunder boomed
The rain spilled
The lake filled

The water ran
A river began
The rain poured
The level soared

It flooded, then
Dried up again
The sun baked
The earth flaked

Everything browned
On the ground
And withered away
On the hottest day

And later on
The sun was gone
For the wind blew
Strong and true

And no surprise
Before my eyes
The clouds loomed
The thunder boomed

Trumpet Lesson

The trumpet looks like
Fun to play
And I'm gonna take lessons
Beginning today

And if I simply live by
My first rule of thumb
The more I practice
The better I'll become

Got a brand-new trumpet
And I'm ready to begin
But first, I gotta figure out
Where to plug it in?

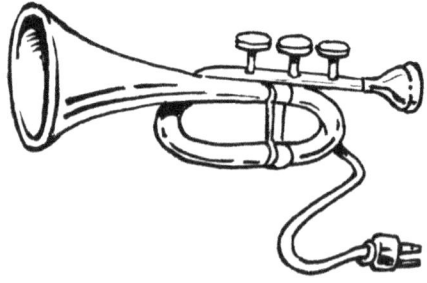

Gravity

The gravity effect
Is constant and true
It's there when we're doing
Whatever we do

It's there to protect us
From floating away
It's there to tell all of us
We're here to stay

It has no perimeter
There isn't a sequel
It's a force that considers
Everything equal

It has no boundaries
It has no borders
It does what it wants
It doesn't take orders

And we barely notice
This unseen force
But it steers our rudder
And governs our course

It never grows weary
It never gets old
Gravity's in charge
So we do as we're told

We can't stop it
We can't start it
Fight it
Rewrite it
Or even outsmart it

We can't alter it

We can't change it

Move it

Disprove it

Or rearrange it

It's gravity's effect

It's constant and true

It's there when we're doing

Whatever we do

There Goes a Bee

There goes a bee
To somewhere unknown
Maybe to someplace
That he's never flown

Maybe he's flying
Where he never flew
For he may well have
Nothing better to do

Perhaps he's heading
Towards fields of flowers
That bloomed from the drenching
Of numerous showers

Looks like he flew
In a southern direction
For he feels the climate
Is a better selection

Or perhaps he's looking
For some of his friends
Could this be the case?
It all depends

It depends on which
It depends on whether
He's looking for friends
Or suitable weather

Depends on the motive
Depends on the source
Depends on the overall
Direction, of course

And all I can see
From the direction he's flown
Is there goes a bee
To somewhere unknown

The Outside World

I was sailing along on the ocean blue
When I suddenly started sinking
I had to think fast
Or I wouldn't last
That's exactly what I was thinking

I called for help on the radio first
But that didn't do any good
I jumped from the craft
And into the raft
And grabbed whatever I could

I ended up on this deserted island
Stranded here on a beach

Where any hope of my salvation
Is completely out of reach

The rescue party searched for weeks
To see what they could see
The search plane flew right over my head
But they never spotted me

I've lived out here for a year and a half
Longing for civilization
My anxiety grows
Because nobody knows
My precise location

Fresh air and this perfect weather
You'd think it's a piece of cake
But it's a jungle out here
With limited gear
How much more can I take?

Beginning to fear
I'll always be here
In total isolation
Beginning to hate
My pending fate
And this current situation

I'm stranded here on a deserted island
There's nowhere I can go
How long will I be stuck out here?
Does anybody know?

Am I truly destined to live my life
In this isolated place?
If I could but reach the outside world
But it's simply not the case

Meantime I'll be waiting here
Survival is gonna be tough
If rescue ever comes my way
It won't be soon enough

The Latest Bookbag

Here's the latest bookbag
That everybody's buying
There's room for almost anything
So I bought one for trying

It holds a dozen pencils
And a multi-colored pen
And a hundred different crayons
Seem to fit right in

I threw in some cookies
And every snack I could find
And a sweet bar of chocolate
That I couldn't leave behind

I've got my headphone set
And my cell phone too
In case I get a phone call
That needs to get through

My trading cards here
My model plane there
I jammed in extra jellybeans
But can't remember where

My frisbee absolutely
And my yo-yo is a must
I want to bring my catcher's mitt
So I'll have to readjust

There's room for all my puzzles
There's also room for lunch
And I packed in some bananas
To eat them by the bunch

I've got everything in it
That I could ever commit
In every place available
That it could possibly fit

There's everything I'll ever need
In all the niches and nooks
Now the question is, indeed
Where do I put my books?

The Yard Next Door

There lives a dog
In the yard next door
He doesn't know why
Doesn't know what for

And it doesn't show
But he's in despair
'Cause he doesn't know
Why he's even there

There's no one around
There's nobody near
There's a reason for this
But it ain't too clear

No one plays fetch
No one plays ball
No one pays any
Attention at all

He knows not why
He ended up this way
But it is what it is
What else can I say?

So he sits over there
In this empty space
Not really sure
If he likes this place

Not really sure
What'll happen tomorrow
So he sighs once again
Ignoring his sorrow

And he doesn't know why
Doesn't know what for
He's only the dog
In the yard next door

If Only the Ice

Ice works great
Isn't it true?
If it wasn't for ice
Then what would we do?

We would soon have to face
The obvious assumption
That drinks wouldn't be fit
For human consumption

For the ice brings about
A chilling sensation
As long as the ice
Can withstand the duration

It chills the food
That would otherwise spoil
It cools the water
That would otherwise boil

Ice works fine
At cooling my drink
And freezing my brain
When I'm trying to think

It chills in the freezer
No argument there
When the power goes out
There's little to spare

And ice works well
At reducing the swelling
What else can it do?
There's really no telling

Ice is unique
For so many things
And the people rejoice
At the elation it brings

It's all too convenient
I don't disagree
It benefits you
It benefits me

It gleams like a crystal
It's cold to the touch
And it's almost insane
That we need it so much

It is a necessity
And without a doubt
Ice is the one thing
We can't do without

It's full potential
Has yet to unfold
Now, if only the ice
Wasn't so cold

Fear Itself

In a spooky castle
In a haunted place
Your heart accelerates
At a frantic pace

You venture on
Your blood is racing
With no idea
What you'll be facing

This place is filled
With historical crimes
That remind us all
Of the worst of times

For this is a castle
Known to be haunted
But you aim to appear
Completely undaunted

You're sensing a presence
That cannot be seen
You're noticing something
If you know what I mean

You hear a sound
So you pause, and then
You focus in on it
And hear it again

It sounded scary
So, your tempo slows
From the hair on your head
To the hair on your toes

The room is cold
And midnight is near
And you hear something else
But what do you hear?

It's so unfamiliar
It's completely unknown
It's sort of a grunt
But it's sort of a groan

It's fear you hear
It's a spirit that's lurking
You try to ignore it
But it isn't working

Creepy apparitions
Slip through the cracks
You bite your lip
You stop in your tracks

This is usually
The human reaction
In a room that features
This sort of distraction

This is awareness
In its purest form
This is so typical
This is the norm

You want to stay put
But you persevere
In an awkward effort
To conquer your fear

And so, as you conquer
You're finding that now
Your innermost phobia
Has vanished somehow

And the fear that controlled you
Controls you no more
And those spooks cannot haunt you
Like they haunted before

So put all those worries
Up high on a shelf
You've nothing to fear
But fear itself

When You Pour Salt

Salt on your ice cream
Makes it taste so delicious
But also makes everyone else
Quite suspicious

For they all believe
The normal assumption
That it's not fit
For human consumption

You'll get strange looks
And comments too
Like "What in the world
Are you trying to do?"

They'll rally in protest
All over the land
Now that you're doing something
They can't understand

But don't pay attention
To whatever they say
Pour salt on your ice cream
At least once a day

Sprinkle it lightly
If you so elect
Or pour it on strong
For a different effect

Ice cream so tasty
And so good to eat
A delightful blend
Both salty and sweet

You'll soon be enjoying
Flavors unknown
When you pour salt
On an ice cream cone

When You're a Mom

Through all the chaos
And through all the calm
You remain dedicated
When you're a mom

When you're a mom
You wipe up the messes
You patch up the pants
And sew all the dresses

You dry bloody noses
And take care of bruises
You drop off the kids
For overnight snoozes

No compensation
For mopping the floor
No pay for the dirt
You sweep out the door

You engage in sports
You normally shouldn't
And you take some chances
You normally wouldn't

You mend broken hearts
And bicycle chains
The pieces and parts
The aches and the pains

And kids nowadays
Show little respect
If you think I'm right
Then you are correct

And they'll cause trouble
Behind your back
So much so
That it's hard to keep track

They have an objective
And this is their plan
To try to get away
With whatever they can

They're twice as kooky
And three times as wild
As you were back then
When you were a child

So you govern the roost
That's all there is to it
It's all you can do
If you wanna get through it

And you often wonder
If anyone cares
Because they're all busy
With their own affairs

Motherhood begins
With a brief introduction
Then it continues
With little instruction

This is your job
Your primary mission
And nothing you do
Can reverse your position

Through all the chaos
You still remain calm
But that's how it goes
When you're a mom

The Truth of It Is

When it comes to smarts
This is my story
I think I was robbed
In the brains category

How do I execute
Logical thinking
If it doesn't come easy
As eating and drinking?

To comprehend theory
Is completely absurd
Like some foreign language
That I've never heard

The grasp of a concept
I'll never achieve
It seems to be something
I cannot conceive

I flounder around
Both dizzy and dense
While everyone else
Uses plain common sense

Me use logic?
Don't make me laugh
My process of thought
Takes a day and a half

I strive for the highest
But the truth of it is
I score the lowest
On the simplest quiz

When it comes to smarts
I'm not like the rest
It's over my head
But I'm doing my best

As The Day Is Long

The key to being right
Is never being wrong
It's part of being humble
It's how I get along

I'm always right
But I don't show it
If I'm ever wrong
Then I don't know it

I aim for solutions
And I never miss
And I think I've discovered
The reason for this

First, I decipher
Where the answer lies
Sometimes it's hidden
In front of my eyes

It's easy to find
If you know where to look
Like the answers you find
In the back of a book

Sometimes it's obvious
Sometimes it's not
Sometimes it's nearly
Impossible to spot

And I've been correct
Throughout my career
You won't find anything
Wrong around here

I'm free of mistakes
As the day is long
Because the key to being right
Is never being wrong

Stone In My Boot

Got a stone in my boot
Down around the heel
And I don't like the way
It's making me feel

It alters my stride
In ways that it shouldn't
It's making me step
Like I normally wouldn't

Tried stomping
Tried shaking
Tried shouting it out
What's all this
'Stone in my boot thing about?'

It's driving me crazy
It's been there too long
There's a stone in my boot
That doesn't belong

It's creating an issue
It's pinching a nerve
This is a punishment
I do not deserve

There's a stone in my boot
And it's rather annoying
It's become a dilemma
That I'm not enjoying

It's quite a predicament
So my primary mission
Is dislodging the stone
From its current position

And as soon as it's gone
I can mosey along
But for now, there's a stone
Where it doesn't belong

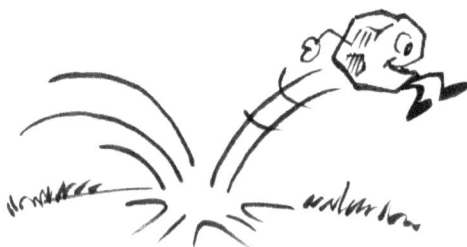

Pencils Are Everywhere

Here I sit without a pencil
To write myself a note
So I can recall on another day
Exactly what I wrote

I simply want to write it down
So later, I can read it
But I never seem to have a pencil
When I really need it

There's never one to borrow
There's never one to use
Will there be one tomorrow
To c hronicle my views?

I've looked all over
But I still don't see
A pencil in a spot
Where a pencil oughta be

I'd search all night
If time would allow
And all day tomorrow
But I need one now!

A pencil for writing
A spontaneous quote
Or whenever I need
To jot down a note

A pencil for using
At a time of my choosing
A pencil to keep
For a day without losing

Pencils are useful
But never around
Pencils are everywhere
But none to be found

It's a normal predicament
So keep this in mind
Pencils are everywhere
But they're hard to find

Never Poke Your Finger

You must obey the rules
It's easy if you try
And never ever ever
Poke your finger in your eye

Never take the crooked road
When the straighter one will do
It's easier to manage
On the latter of the two

Never take advice
From an idiotic fool
He's the one who always failed
At everything in school

And never ever cast your eye
Directly towards the sun
Or promise someone two
When all you have is one

Never take the city bus
When you have a taxi waiting
Sometimes tempers flair
And can thus be irritating

Always hire someone
Who dresses for the job
And never hire anyone
Who dresses like a slob

Never wake a sleeping dog
In the middle of a dream
This suggestion stands to reason
Or so it would seem

Never spill the milk
And cry about it after
Overcome the overflow
With a bit of laughter

Never bet the horse
Who cannot win the race
He'll be the one who cannot seem
To keep up with the pace

Never run the halls
With scissors in your hand
Or lounge around the beach
Then complain about the sand

Never do tomorrow
What you can do today
It is the better method
It is the better way

Take these rules and keep them
You'll have the upper hand
And when you find their reasoning
Then you'll understand

Rules are to be followed
Let me make it clear
So follow all the rules
If you want to function here

Obey the rules
Avoid the fools
And let me clarify
Never ever ever
Poke your finger
In your eye

Igloo

I had to build an igloo
Just to stay alive
It's something that I had to do
In order to survive

'Cause in the desert
It gets so hot
In order to survive
You have to build an igloo
Just to stay alive

Without A Poet

Without a poet
What would we do?
We'd stumble through pages
With never a clue

No artful crafting
No rhythm or rhyme
And this would confuse us
Most of the time

We'd live in a world
Of complete disarray
With no one to lead us
Or show us the way

I'm delighted we have
A poet like you
Because, without a poet
What would we do?

The Corner of My Eye

I watched two clouds
From the corner of my eye
And how different they were
When creeping on by

I saw a couple more
Floating later in the day
Slipping through the sky
In a similar way

Every cloud I see
Has in common with the other
Something coincidental
And likewise, with another

And then it dawned upon me
And I focused my attention
Observing something obvious
I think that I should mention

I noticed from a distance
Out of the corner of my eye
That no two clouds are identical
When creeping on by

The Neighbors

I live next to an old graveyard
And yes, it can be scary
And you might say
There ain't no way
I'd live by a cemetery

'Cause I've been told
The stories of old
And how I should live in fear
From the absence of light
When it's real late at night
And the tombstones ever so near

But there's little chance
In this circumstance
Of hearing a haunting sound
Or even a sight
Of a ghost in the night
Or spirits roaming around

There's nothing to fear
About living out here
But you won't know 'til you try it
Not many would stay
But hey, that's okay
At least my neighbors are quiet

I Didn't Mean to Lean

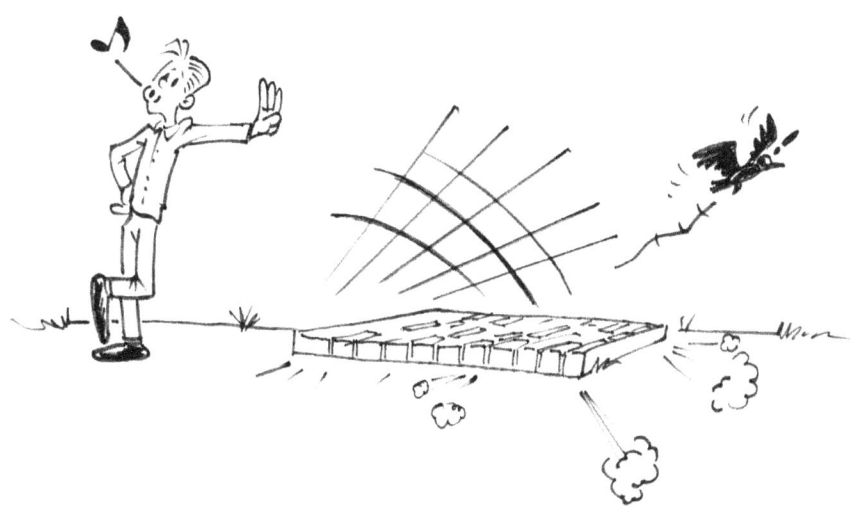

I leaned upon an ancient wall
That soon began to tip and fall
What once had stood
So straight and tall
Is no longer standing there at all

Everyone Was Nine

Everyone was nine
That's ever been ten
That's the bottom line
Again and again

And everyone was eight
That's ever been nine
So there's no debate
And it's perfectly fine

And seven I'm told
And six, five and four
Can't be that old
And not younger before

And you can't be three
If you never were two
It could never be
And it would never do

And two and not one
Or one and not none
Let's face the facts
It couldn't be done

So whatever you've been
Is perfectly fine
But you cannot be ten
Unless you were nine

A Thousand Pounds of Hay

Once a farmer's plowing cow
Ate a thousand pounds of hay somehow
And grew so large in fact, that now
She's much too big to pull the plow

So the farmer now must pull the plow
And till the soil by the sweat of his brow
All because the plowing cow
Ate a thousand pounds of hay, somehow

The Wild Wild West

Years ago

When times were best

Way way back

In the wild wild west

There were gamblers and ramblers

And swindlers, and more

Buffalo jerky

And banjos galore

Five-card draw
And poker all night
Half of them cheat
And half of them fight

Dirt on your boot
And mud in your eye
And horse manure
In ample supply

A prospector's claim
To fortune and fame
Coyotes and cattle
And men in a saddle

Rodeos and roundups
And festive jamborees
Ten-gallon hats
And plain dungarees

Rickety wagons
On dusty trails
Pesky flies
And horses' tails

Those were the days
Of the one room school
Of the town saloon
And the two-bit mule

Square dancing was common
For the ladies and men
That's how it was done
When it was done back then

Constantly sweating
From a day so hot
One bath a month
If you need it or not

Gunslingers and feuding
All going down
And shootouts were common
In the middle of town

Sheriffs and marshals
Would try to get rid
Of desperate outlaws
Like Billy the Kid

The blacksmith, the doctor
And the rancher were men
Who all played their part
In the west back then

Study your history
And soon you will learn
That those were the times
That'll never return

Those were the times
When the times were best
Way way back
In the wild wild west

We Eat Barbeque

We eat barbeque
More than we should
It's all because barbeque
Tastes so good

It's not on account
Of a price within reason
It's not on account
Of the barbeque season

It's not on account
Of the flavor we savor
It's more on account
Of its hypnotic flavor

It's not because everyone
Seems to be hooked
It's simply because of
The way that it's cooked

It's all for the taste
And the barbeque sauce
It's everyone's gain
And nobody's loss

It's all because barbeque
Tastes so good
That we eat barbeque
More than we should

Pots And Pans

Pots are made to bing
Pans are made to bang
Not so much to cling
But more or less to clang

Pots are made to ding
Pans are made to dong
Not so much to ping
But more or less to pong

Mothers won't condone it
But that's a mother's call
Fathers won't accept it
For very long at all

To us it's a noise
We really enjoy
To them, the ruckus
Can only annoy

And the more we bang
The more it perturbs
And the more we clang
The more it disturbs

And pots and pans
That disturb, indeed
Are pots and pans
They do not need

But pots and pans
Are fun to bang
They're fun to cling
And fun to clang

The perfect thing
To have around
To clang and cling
To bang and pound

Left hand, right hand
Fast or slow
On and on
And on I'll go

Rain or shine
It matters not
Freezing cold
Or blazing hot

Sun that shines
Or clouds of gray
I bang my pots and pans
And say:

"It doesn't matter
The way or the weather
Bang your pots
And pans together!"

Mathematics

Zero plus zero
Is zero, I know
Nothing more, nothing less
Understandably so

You add nothing here
Subtract nothing there
And still you have nothing
At all anywhere

You take away nothing
From nothing at all
And you have a number
That's incredibly small

No pencil required
No pen filled with ink
It's a formula that isn't
As hard as you think

A novice solution
An elementary task
Could it be this simple?
You don't have to ask

There's two plus two
And one plus one
But no math is as simple
As nothing plus none

You won't need algebra
On this present occasion
And no need for calculus
To solve this equation

No call for an abacus
Invading the scene
No division required
Or adding machine

No matter the method
How simple it seems
Could ever be easier
In your wildest dreams

From kindergarten class
To a college dorm
That's mathematics
In its simplest form

It Always Pays

I look both ways
Before crossing the street
Up to the clouds
Then down at my feet

I look one way
Then I look the other
It's the way I was told
To do it by Mother

First, I glance towards the sky
And wait for traffic to pass me by
Then I peer towards my toes
Between my feet
And around my nose

Adjustments are made
And necessary corrections
It's habit for me
To look both directions

And when it's clear
Then I make my move
There's nothing here
I'm trying to prove

So now you know
Wherever you go
Look up, then down at your feet
It always pays
To look both ways
Before you cross the street

A Hole to China

I wanted to go to China
But I couldn't find a ride
So I started walking around the planet
To reach the other side

I knew the trip would take some time
I grabbed my favorite shoes
A backpack with necessities
And things that I could use

I hadn't traveled far at all
When blisters soon appeared
And all the pain that I imagined
Was worse than I had feared

It soon became a journey
That I could not complete
Because it seemed the more I walked
The more it hurt my feet

And I began to realize
If I'm to reach my goal
All I really had to do
Was dig a perfect hole

I'd have to bore straight through the Earth
Starting from the ground
This direction is so much shorter
Than traveling around

I started digging frantically
The outcome was the same
For the deeper that I dug the hole
The harder it became

I want to go to China
But I'm going about it wrong
This direction is half the distance
But it's taking twice as long

I don't care how hard it gets
I've already come this far
Sometimes we'd rather be someplace
Other than we are

Weird People

Weird people are strange
Strange people are weird
And all throughout society
These people are feared

They don't get along
And they don't fit in
And the public is antsy
Again and again

They're viewed as an outcast
And revered by so many
In need of direction
But not furnished with any

We find their actions
Unwelcome and loathing
Peculiar individuals
In abnormal clothing

We could hang out together
But nobody will
They'll move along
While we stand still

We keep our distance
And they keep theirs
We could all be friends
But nobody dares

So they carry on
These people so feared
Weird people are strange
Strange people are weird

Me Against the Clock

I came upon a tunnel
A shortcut through the rock
I'm always in a hurry
It's me against the clock

The choices now before me
Are either one of two
Such a tough decision
So what am I to do?

Take the time to walk around
The giant rock for free
Or venture through the tunnel
And pay a simple fee?

They only charge a ten-cent toll

'Cause that's the going price

I only have to pay it once

But now I'm thinking twice

For a cave collapse would leave me

In a heaping hunk of trouble

And they would have to dig me out

Of a heaping pile of rubble

But if I take the extra time

It takes to walk around

It would take me twice as long

To cover all the ground

Take the chance

And spend a dime

Or play it safe

But lose the time?

I can either go around

Or shortcut through the rock

I'm always in a hurry

It's me against the clock

The Olden Days

What was it like
In the olden days?
Everyone focused
And set in their ways

They walked to school
They did the chores
They spent their money
In the ten-cent stores

No instant messages
No instant text
And nobody then
Knew what was next

Ten-pound telephones
Mounted to the wall
Only one television
If you had one at all

And telegraph lines
Spanned the land
When Morse code
Was in command

Roll up windows
Were never tinted
The internet, too
Wasn't invented

Topcoats, high collars
And a t-strap heel
Ladies' cloche hats
Had broad appeal

Argyle socks
Were the perfect style
And you physically tuned
The radio dial

Carnations adorned
A tuxedo's lapel
Those were the times
I remember so well

Times were simple
But work was hard
And nobody needed
A debit card

Everyone focused
And set in their ways
That's how it was
In the olden days

Like It or Not...

It's dark
It's light
It's day
It's night

It's cold
It's hot
It's raining
It's not

It's hot
It's cold
It's not
Controlled

It's dim
It's bright
It's a clear
Twilight

It's windy
It's still
With a bit
Of a chill

It's wet
It's dry
It's because
Of the sky

It's sunny
It's mild
It's calm
It's wild

It's natural
That's all
It's spring
It's fall

It changes
A lot
Like it
Or not

It's take
It's give
It's how
We live

If It's Worth a Nickel

I have a nickel
A nickel to spend
What will I purchase?
This will depend

This will depend
Upon whether or not
I should be spending
The nickel I've got

Some things I know
Cannot be bought
But a nickel is worth
A little more than I thought

So what will I purchase?
How should I know?
A nickel won't buy
What it bought long ago

I'll make a decision
By the end of the day
But I will not fritter
This fortune away

But it must be spent
It's what I must do
Should I buy something old
Or buy something new?

It really doesn't matter
As long as it's spent
Later I'll ponder
Where the money all went

My decision on this
Is a tiny bit fickle
But it's worth five cents
If it's worth a nickel

Fairly Unstable

She could be a ballerina
Or an overnight sensation
If only she could focus
On a bit of concentration

She could thrill the audience
If given a chance
And leave them astounded
If she could dance

She could be a professional
On any given day
If those two feet
Didn't get in the way

She hopes in earnest
To become a success
But her balance is off
She tries nonetheless

She could twirl like the wind
In a symphonic display
If there were some formula
To show her the way

She's stylishly clumsy
And she's dreadfully certain
That she'll never see
The opening curtain

Yet, she doesn't give up
Her efforts are gallant
It's an awkward display
Of one with no talent

She's no Ginger Rogers
She's no Fred Astaire
She longs for the talent
But life isn't fair

But she loves dancing
So how will she learn?
Her lack of ability
Is a major concern

She could be a ballerina
If only she was able
But she's perfectly clumsy
And fairly unstable

Big Feet Ain't Small

Big feet ain't bad
Big feet ain't bad
Big feet are all
I've ever had

My feet are big
Not tiny at all
My feet ain't little
My feet ain't small

And people stare
When first we meet
And they can't stop looking
At my two feet

I like to snack
And I like to eat
But it all goes down
To my two feet

I don't take chances
And I don't drive
Because I'm not sure
If I'll come back alive

And it's tough for me
To walk the street
And to go unnoticed
With these two feet

And I don't dance
Nor do I ski
Not with these feet
At the bottom of me

My wardrobe
Is actually incomplete
'Cause they don't make shoes
To fit these feet

When you're built like me
Your choices are few
In what you can try
And what you can do

Big feet ain't bad
They're actually good
I think my feet
Are misunderstood

Big Feet ain't bad
Ain't bad at all
Only thing is
Big feet ain't small

My Sister's Teeth

My sister never brushed her teeth
When she was growing up
Nor rinsed her mouth with fluoride
From a single paper cup

Now her teeth spend every night
Soaking in a cup
Because my sister never brushed her teeth
When she was growing up

Ox In a Box

An ox inside a box
Would have difficulty grazing
But a box inside an ox
Would truly be amazing

A Prickly Porcupine

If you kiss a prickly porcupine
Upon his prickly cheek
I doubt you'll kiss another one
For at least another week

The Lazy Sheriff

In the heart of Oklahoma
Back in eighteen sixty-five
The sheriff running Edmon County
Was the laziest man alive

He sat all day sipping lemonade
And napping in a chair
A lazy man with no concern
A man without a care

Then forty bandits came to town
Riding like the dickens
They knew the sheriff was a lazy man
And the town was easy pickins'

They robbed the bank
And took the cash
Like bandits often do
And like a crook
The bandits took
The gold and silver too

The ranchers had their horses taken
Then they swiped their cows
The farmers saw their mules were gone
And someone stole their plows!

They only left behind
The things they couldn't haul
But the sheriff didn't seem to care
Very much at all

He said, "Now if bandits come to town
It ain't that big a deal
'Cause there's nothing left in Edmon County
For anyone to steal."

Ice Skating

Cathy Bates

Put on her skates

To do a little skating

Though a winter day

Was months away

Cathy was tired of waiting

She started off

Across the lake

But sank down to her knees

She wants to skate

But has to wait

Because it's seventy-five degrees

To Be Very Little

Meatball the dog
Too big for his skin
Too big for himself
And the body he's in

Too big of a neck
On too big of a beast
Too big for his collar
To say the least

He can't take walks
For his collar's too small
I know about this
Because he's tried them all

He's too big to train
And too big for tricks
Too big to scratch
The fleas and the ticks

Too big for the floor
Too big for a lap
Too loud of a snore
When taking a nap

Too big to cuddle
Too big to hug
Too big of a puddle
Right on the rug

Though not too big
To create disarray
Which Meatball achieves
Throughout the day

But too big to vilify
And too big to scold
Too big to insist
To do as he's told

One gulp to drink
One bite to feed
Too big I think
Too big indeed

Too big all around
Too big to the core
Meatball's too big
To be small anymore

Too big overall
And too big to be
Too bad for Meatball
As you can see

Too big up the side
Too big down the middle
Meatball's too big
To be very little

The Bigger I Become

It goes to prove
The more I eat
The bigger I become
And I can say
I got this way
By eating more than some

By consuming all I can
I fill my hungry belly
With everything
From fries to pies
And homemade bread and jelly

I eat so much
And I eat so fast
That forks and spoons
And knives don't last

Utensils are of little use
And the dishes obsolete
The table sags from all the weight
Of everything I eat

You'll find nothing in the pantry
In the freezer, very little
Only scraps within the fryer
Even less upon the griddle

That's because there's nothing left
After I get done
That's because I never leave
Any food for anyone

Eating for the sake of taste
Is really not the aim
Because when you eat as much as I
It all tastes the same

Nevertheless, I'm eating more
I'm eating more than some
Which goes to prove
The more I eat
The bigger I become

Twice As Much Traffic

There's twice as much traffic
As an hour ago
And when it will end?
I do not know

And I do not know
What causes the streets
To become congested
While my car overheats

And my car overheats
The longer it sits
And the longer it idles
The hotter it gets

And the hotter it gets
The worse it'll run
A combination of idling
And the heat of the sun

And the heat of the sun
And the current situation
Is the primary reason
Of all this frustration

And all this frustration
Is one more reason
My car overheats
Throughout the season

And throughout the season
It all depends
On the volume of traffic
And where it all ends

And where it all ends
I do not know
There's twice as much traffic
As an hour ago

Used Socks

Selling used socks
Gets tougher each day
I practically have to
Give them away

I bought several dozen
In a business transaction
Which led to my ultimate
Dissatisfaction

And I had no clue
It would be this tough
But I thought I could do it
If I tried hard enough

Little did I know
It would take this long
Was I ever mistaken
Was I ever wrong

I thought used socks
Would be easy to sell
Even full of holes
And a gut-wrenching smell

They're not the best choice
They're not even new
But if you're in a pinch
Believe me, they'll do

I realize they're dirty
And I know they smell
And that makes it difficult
For anyone to sell

They're filled with rips
They're plagued with holes
From the top to the tips
And down to the soles

They're no good to the public
There's nothing appealing
They'll stink up your shoes
They'll stick to the ceiling

They're no good to anyone
They're useless indeed
Used socks are the socks
That no one will need

It's pointless to hope
For it's hopeless to try
Used socks are the socks
That no one will buy

I've filled no orders
I can't cover the cost
And you wouldn't believe
The money I've lost

I suppose I'm destined
To give them away
'Cause selling used socks
Ain't going my way

Afternoon Nap

In the year nineteen-hundred
He laid down his head
For an afternoon nap
In his warm little bed

All cozy and snug
Under covers he lay
As an afternoon nap
Soon filled the day

And the day spent napping
Then became two
Until another and another
Became quite a few

And the days turned to weeks
Then the months went fast
And he kept on napping
As the years slid past

After ninety-nine years
The alarm clock dinging
He opened his eyes
While it sat there ringing

Well rested, he said
"It's surprising to see
How refreshing
An afternoon nap can be"

The Pen the Finger and Thumb

Put down your thoughts
Whenever they come
Using the pen
The finger and thumb

Ideas that linger
In the back of your head
Write them all down
So they can be read

Thoughts that meander
In a maze of perception
A theory perceived
from the pits of conception

Lyrics that flow
Deep from within
Like music that's played
Through an old violin

A creative barrage
Like no one has seen
Like a rambling ball
In a pinball machine

Like a blistering wind
In the heart of a twister
Or a flurry of signals
Through a modern transistor

So write down whatever
Your head visualizes
And your mind
You will find
Is full of surprises

Subtle notations
Will be all the rage
Line after line
Page after page

The pen you will find
Governs the ink
The heart of your mind
Reveals what you think

But is it the ink
Or the mind that's the key?
Whatever you think
Is what it'll be

The Tide

As the tide ebbs
And tide flows
The water comes
The water goes

The moon dims
And then glows
The ocean tos
The ocean fros

Momentum hurries
Momentum slows
As the world spins
The wind blows

And all the turbulence
It undergoes
Forces unite
And then oppose

Let's me see why
I suppose
The tide ebbs
The tide flows

High Road Low Road

High road, low road
How should I choose?
Either way forward
I'm destined to lose

This way or that way
What should I do?
How do I choose
Between one of the two?

There is no hint
There is no clue
The choices are limited
And selections are few

I'm torn between this road
Or taking the next
The decision before me
Has me perplexed

But I will decide
And then when I do
That will decide it
And cover it too

Either way forward
I'm destined to lose
High road, low road
How should I choose?

Quite Certain

I sat in a chair
That wasn't there
I ended up
Down on the floor

I knew right then
That never again
Would I sit
In that chair anymore

Ten Foot Two

Stanley McCue
Stands ten foot two
He's the tallest boy I know
Even the tallest man on the block
Stands several feet below

He's taller than you
He's taller than me
And what a sight to behold
He's taller than anyone
Ever should be
And he's only twelve years old

He barely fits on the bus in the morning
He can hardly walk down the hall
"I've got knots on my head
From the ceiling," he said
"And my desk is way too small"

"My pants don't fit
My sleeves' too short
And these shoes are killing my feet

All the clothes
From my head to my toes
Are completely obsolete"

He's high as a building
He's tall as a tower
He's too big to fit
In a typical shower

And he knows, not at all
Why he grew so high
Though he knows he's tall
But he doesn't know why

He bangs into this
He bumps into that
It's not uncommon
To knock off his hat

Some people snicker
And some people laugh
Some say he looks
Like a human giraffe

He's ten foot two
From hat to shoe
And still a growing lad
And that's not all
If you think he's tall
You oughta see his dad

The Man of Steel

Is Superman invincible?
Let me fill you in
He's always had a weakness
That's always how it's been

He's quite formidable
In his bright red cape
It's an image from which
He cannot escape

His suit is blue
His boots are red
And he has some trouble
Seeing through lead

But he has a weakness
That nobody knows
It isn't too obvious
And it never shows

He's strong as an ox
He's faster than fast
But he has some issues
From back in the past

It's not what you think
Or what you thought to be true
It's actually something
That you never knew

If you thought it was kryptonite
If you thought this was so
Then obviously there's something
Else you should know

He's not afraid
Of a Great White Shark
But sources tell me
He's afraid of the dark

The invincible hero
Of the U.S.A.
The immortal legend
From so far away

Faster than a bullet
That speeds through the air
But go out after dark?
He wouldn't dare

He leaps tall buildings
In a single bound
But courage at bedtime
Cannot be found

Not one locomotive
Can match his might
But he won't be pushing
Locomotives tonight

His last name Kent
His first name Clark
But whoever knew
He was scared of the dark?

A Bowl of Cement

Add half a cup of H_2O
To a bowl of dry cement
Stir the mixture nice and slow
'Til it turns to sediment

Pour in a pound of desert sand
Grind in some gravel and grit
Smooth out the lumps
With the spoon in your hand
And mix it up a bit

Now sprinkle salt into the bowl
Like you've never sprinkled before
The exceptional taste
Won't go to waste
So what are you waiting for?

Let it begin to dry, and then
It's almost ready to serve
And after it's dry
It's ready to try
If you've gathered up the nerve

A bowl of cement
Is for those who are willing
To try out something new
And a bowl of cement
Is certainly filling
But awful tough to chew

All Mistakes Collectively

My feet are really hurting
My shoes are kinda tight
'Cause my right is where
My left should be
And my left is on the right

It's difficult to walk like this
There must be something I can do
If only there were guidelines
On how to wear a shoe

I've made mistakes before
This is surely not the first
But of all mistakes collectively
This has got to be the worst

A Clap of Thunder

A clap of thunder
Is mighty loud
But seldom ever seen
Sounds to me like
A clap of thunder
Is only a noise machine

And if you stand under
A clap of thunder
You'll discover what I mean
That a clap of thunder
Is mighty loud
But seldom ever seen

Lifelong Search

One may search
A lifetime's worth
Of happiness
Here upon this earth

And never find
A single thing
That'll bring more joy
Than a friend can bring

O'Brien Street

There's a mailbox down O'Brien Street
Third house on the right
Looking for some mail to eat
To curb his appetite

No matter how much mail he eats
It's never quite enough
Even if he crams his belly
With packages and stuff

When the mailman approached
The mailbox devised
A clever little plan
And the mailbox set his sights upon
The unsuspecting man

And before the mailman knew it
The mailbox grabbed him by his coat
He gobbled up the mailman
And shoved him down his throat

Now he waits all day
The identical way
'Til someone else passes by
And there's danger, I say
If you walk that way
So keep an open eye

Or you may soon become obsolete
And vanish out of sight
As you walk along O'Brien Street
Third house on the right

Green Paint

Green is now my favorite color
And no other color will do
I only like the color green
Not yellow, red or blue

So I use green paint
To paint everything green
From the top to the bottom
And down in between

Everything that wasn't green
Was painted right away
If it wasn't green the day before
It'll be green today

Now everything is finally green
From the ceiling to the floor
And I don't have to paint
Things green anymore

So when you're free to color
With absolutely no restraint
Take it from an expert
Use green paint

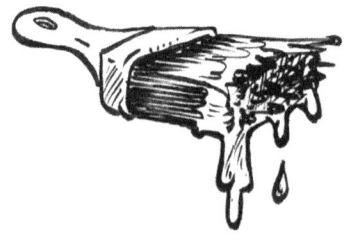

They Don't Make Shovels

I thought I bought the perfect shovel
To dig the perfect hole
A perfect metal spade attached
To a perfect wooden pole

But the tip's at the bottom
And the spade's up top
Not like they were before
I wonder sometimes
Why they don't make shovels
Like they used to anymore?

The Jump Rope Dope

Someone there is jumping rope
Someone there looks like a dope
Someone there doesn't care
That the rope's not spinning
Through the air

Someone there up in the air
Doesn't have a single care
And all that someone wants to do
Is jump the rope that's laying there

Frontwards backwards, up and down
Jumping back and forth
Jumping rope from east to west
Jumping south to north

Jumping rope, rain or shine
Jumping high and low
Jumping by his own design
As high as he can go

And I've seen kids jump rope before
In a suburban habitat
But I have never
Seen anybody ever
Ever jump rope like that

It Doesn't Take Long

It has to be the shortest song
I think I've ever heard
It only has one note to hear
It only has one word

It doesn't take long
To hear this song
And not much practice
To sing along

So listen close
To the radio
It could pass right by
And you'd never know

It's the shortest song
To reach number one
And once it starts
It's already done

A Gust of Wind

The wind swooped in
From out of the blue
I began to spin
And away I flew

It spun me
And twirled me
It turned me around
It whipped me
It whirled me
Down to the ground

And I ended up
Flat on my face
And the wind disappeared
Without a trace

I'm peeling my eyes
From here on in
So the wind doesn't sneak up
On me again

The Hair up There

"Look at your head"
The barber said
"The top is slick and bare
There's nothing but skin
Where strands have been
And no sign of any hair"

I simply said
"Look back at my head
There's hair on either side
A full head of hair
Is still up there
I just part it very wide"

A Black Tuxedo

Randy rented a black tuxedo
To wear to the prom tonight
But he ended up renting
The very last one
And it didn't fit Randy right

It all begins at six-fifteen
And Randy can't be late
But he can't get
The clothing to fit
Or his tie to line up straight

His pants are too long
And too loose through the hips
And the sleeves reach far beyond
Randy's fingertips

He said, "I've got a couple hours
But the time won't last
I'd better think of something
And think of something fast"

"Or my legs need to grow
A foot and a half
To avoid an awkward scene
And my arms need to stretch out
Farther than that
Between now and six-fifteen"

Willie's Luggage

Willie took a trip
But Willie didn't pack
Willie wore thirteen
Suits on his back

"I don't trust the airline
With my luggage," Willie said
"I don't trust them with my clothes
So I'm wearing them instead"

They lost Willie's luggage
A hundred times before
But they're not gonna lose
Willie's luggage anymore

The Ultimate Coaster

It's the fastest
It's the tallest
It's the biggest
Not the smallest
Rollercoaster ever made
It's fifteen miles
From start to finish
And the fastest track ever laid

It stands over twelve hundred

Feet in the air

And once you reach the top

You wonder exactly

What you're doing up there

As your ears begin to pop

You look around

At the people on the ground

Who look incredibly small

You crest the peak

And your knees get weak

As you suddenly start to fall

And you soon find out

From the top of it all

You're higher than The Eiffel Tower

Faster and faster

And faster you fall

At three hundred miles an hour

You shoot around the bend
You bank to the side
You never loosen your grip
You're gliding with ease
With your knees
In the breeze
On a most fantastic trip

It's the ultimate coaster
It's the ultimate thrill
It's the maximum in pure
Roller coaster overkill

It's the greatest
It's the wildest
It's the scariest
Not the mildest
It's the number one
Coaster nationwide

It's a whole lot more
Than any coaster before
But no one
Has the courage to ride

A Sleeping Forest

A steady wind began to blow
And one tree whispered soft and low
The branches swayed from left to right
It was certainly a soothing site

Soon I heard a dozen trees
Singing softly in the breeze
And as they sang their lazy song
Some others joined to sing along

'Til every tree my eye could see
Was singing perfect harmony
But all great songs will surely end
As did the trees in the dying wind

But the wind, in time will stir and then
A sleeping forest will sing again
It's amazing what they undergo
When a steady wind decides to blow

If Ever a World There Was

Nancy's busy blowing bubbles
'Cause that's what Nancy does
She's the number one blower of bubbles
If ever there ever was

When she forms a bubble
She cannot ignore
Nancy's ready to blow it
And if Nancy's obsessed
With anything more
Nancy doesn't show it

She's not interested in anything else
For nothing else suits her fancy
Blowing bubbles is the only thing
That has to do with Nancy

She never stops
When it comes to bubbles
Nancy never quits
She's always busy blowing bubbles
Every chance she gets

She lives in a world
Without any troubles
If ever a world there was
And Nancy will always be blowing bubbles
'Cause that's what Nancy does.

No Yo-Yo at All

First take the yo-yo
And then take the string
Wind it up tight
And give it a fling

Down and up
And down again
Flick it just right
And there it'll spin

Flip it and flop it
You won't ever drop it
It'll simply rise and fall

But a yo-yo that isn't

Attached to a string

Is really no yo-yo at all

Hazard Hill

There's danger that can almost kill

When climbing up on Hazard Hill

Most folks won't climb

But still

Some will

Who end up just like

Jack and Jill

Toothpaste

Timmy awoke this morning
And started to brush his teeth
Then the upper teeth began to cling
To the fillings underneath

Only moments later
Timmy found he couldn't chew
Which happens when
Instead of toothpaste
Timmy uses glue

Clyde The Camel

Clyde the camel lives in the desert
Where the air is hot and dry
There ain't no breeze
And there ain't no trees
And water's in short supply

All day long the sun beats down
And burns the barren land
And the only shade you'll ever see
Is your shadow on the sand

Not a cloud in the sky
Goes passing by
But you haven't heard the worst
The lack of rain
On the desert plain
Gives a camel quite a thirst

But somehow Clyde the camel
Seems to always manage
By a solution he uses
At a time that he chooses
That gives him a slight advantage

The other camels seem to think
That Clyde has got it made
If no water's there
He pulls up a chair
And orders lemonade

Tug-O-War

Since I've been playing tug-o-war
I've always understood
That I tug 'til I can tug no more
But it does me little good

I tug with my left hand
I pull with my right
My feet are standing firm
And the rope is good and tight

I've got a grip
That'll never slip
And I'm feeling pretty good
But I don't think I'm playing
Tug-o-war the way I should

Umbrella Malfunction

My umbrella doesn't keep me dry
Like it's supposed to do
And I can honestly testify
There's drizzle in my shoe

Water's dripping down my back
And ruining my dress
And my hundred-dollar hairdo
Is now a total mess

What I cannot figure out is why
It's over my head, and yet
Instead of keeping me nice and dry
It turns me soaking wet

And it's still raining
And I'm still complaining
About this undeniable defect
They should have told me
Before they sold me
An umbrella they couldn't perfect

I'm not going out in the rain
Until I'm really prepared
There's nothing to gain
Out here in the rain
Until this thing is repaired

Rotten Luck

A bolt of lightning struck the ground
Right in my own backyard
It knocked the outdoor furniture around
It must've hit pretty hard

With a flash so bright
It lit the night
In a jiffy it was gone
It didn't hit me
But I could see
It burned a spot on the lawn

Lightning can be dangerous
And perhaps you won't be struck
But if you do
Then this is true
You've got some rotten luck

The odds of getting
Struck by lightning
Are really very slim
But those who have
Say it's certainly frightening
So listen close to them

They say the safest place to be
Is to be where lightning's been
Because wherever a bolt of lightning strikes
It never strikes again

Accidents Can Happen

Accidents can happen
Anytime at any place
Not much we can do about it
It's a fact we have to face

Accidents can happen
Always have and always will
So the best way to avoid one
Is stand completely still

Standing in the Mirror

Standing in the mirror
Is a girl I always see
And when I stare
She's always there
Looking back at me

She's never spoken out her name
But I seem to recognize
Our freckled faces look the same
She's familiar to my eyes

She was there this morning
And here she is again
Our movements seem identical
She could almost be my twin

And I wonder as I stare at her
How long this girl will be
Standing in the mirror
And looking back at me?

A Red Balloon

Floating in a red balloon
Way up where it's high
Can anything be more thrilling
Than soaring through the sky?

Hovering can be so appealing
Looking down at everything
I can't imagine a greater feeling
Than a red balloon can bring

Floating in a red balloon
Soaring all around
I'm eager to go up very soon
But I'm afraid to leave the ground

The Teacher's Pet

All the kids in science class
Are behaving at their best
Because sitting by the teacher
Is a petrifying guest

He's meaner than a monster
He's bigger than a bear
His breath is hot
And he's got a lot
Of black and stringy hair

He doesn't say a word
He's not into having fun
He lurks over there
With a gazing stare
Looking down at everyone

So everyone's behaving
For the teacher you can bet
Because a thousand-pound gorilla
Is now the teacher's pet

A Heavy Fog

A heavy fog rolled through town
And settled all around
It scattered quick
And became so thick
I could barely see the ground

The birds quit singing
The bells stopped ringing
At precisely ten 'til eight
Even the cat
Was as blind as a bat
And the mail was four hours late

Everybody antsy

The whole town nervous

And no one could really relax

The mayor even hid

Like most of us did

And the paperboy stopped in his tracks

Traffic came to a grinding halt

And school was canceled too

Certainly, this was nobody's fault

For what could anyone do?

The sun didn't shine

Until two forty-nine

As the fog pulled away from the ground

And all I can say

Is "What a peculiar day

When a heavy fog rolls around"

The Automatic Homework Machine

I've assembled an automatic
Homework machine
Perfectly safe
Environmentally clean

I crafted the parts
That I used to combine
The machinery that formed
The ingenious design

The simple to operate
Buttons and dials
Gain access to well over
Ten million files

Feed your assignment
Through the incoming bay
Enter the data
And get out of the way

The machine does the rest
It's as simple as that
And out comes your homework
In ten seconds flat

It worked so well
That I built ten more
From mechanisms purchased
At the hardware store

Insurance is standard
And shipping is free
It comes with a standard
Money-back guarantee

So order today
You'll have it by morning
But don't turn it on
'Til you study the warning

Which indicates clearly
In section thirteen
You won't become smarter
If you use this machine

All About Sailing

I started out across the bay
After buying a brand-new boat
I thought she was fine
But this sailboat of mine
Had trouble staying afloat

Within an hour
Came a storm and a shower
The sails became tangled and torn
From the bow to the stern
And around every turn
My boat was weathered and worn

Water came in
Through the cracks by then
And I didn't know what to think
So I had to start bailing
While I was sailing
Hoping the craft wouldn't sink

I sailed all the way
Across Hudson Bay
Throwing water over the side
I was trying to reach
The closest beach
So harder and harder I tried

I finally landed on a sandy shore
Tired, but glad to be there
I sat and I thought
About the boat that I bought
And have only two things to share

The first thing I'll say
After sinking all day
Is, "I've learned a lot about bailing"
And second to share
Is, "I'm completely aware
I know nothing at all about sailing"

Checkered Flag

Welcome all fans

Welcome all fans

To the biggest race of the year

Sit in a seat

Or stand on your feet

Either way, we're glad you're here

A perfect day

The weather's fine

Gentlemen, insert your keys

Line 'em up at the starting line

And start your engines please

Spinning tires and grinding gears
The engines are revving so loud
The fans erupt with roaring cheers
And excitement fills the crowd

Round and round
And round they go
In a tight and tidy pack
Some drive fast
And some drive slow
As they circle around the track

The yellow car's winning
Now the blue car's ahead
But the red car
Is coming up fast
It's all a big test
To see who'll be first
And which one's gonna be last

But it's thoroughly confusing
To watch for hours
This circling caravan
Why race at all
If the goal is to finish
At the same place where you began?

Other Available Works

ABOUT THE AUTHOR

Born, raised, and living in Charleston, SC, Mark first started putting verse in the public eye in the early '80s by using a marquee for a Pizza Hut on Sam Rittenberg Blvd. where he was employed. It was one of those signs where you could slide the hand-sized letters onto the face of the apparatus with a pole. Black letters on a white background made for an easy read, and it lit up so passing traffic could read it at night. Only four lines were available, so he was limited, although his ideas were limitless. It was mainly used to display the pizza specials offered, but that all changed after the manager agreed to let him use it one day for a four-line rhyme. He had some ideas and came up with something silly that would fit up there. He remembers writing it out first on a piece of paper and showing Danny, the manager, for approval, who snickered and said, "Yeah, that's hilarious, go put it up there!" It got to the point where Mark had so many phrases that he could put up different ones on each side of the sign. They were left up there for a week at a time and then swapped for a new one. It went on for several years, and customers would come in for pizza and mention that they found it humorous and would ask, "who's coming up with those funny phrases on the marquee all the time?" and co-workers always pointed to Mark. He kept them recorded in a journal somewhere, but the record of all those four-line phrases have long since vanished.

"I've always found the rhythm of the sentence important and the rhyme at the conclusion most relevant. The challenge of drafting something worth reading intrigues me. The proper placement of a nearly infinite selection of available words within the English language that best suits the theme is the challenge." The application to this as it pertains to writing is similar to aviator Orville Wright, when he said, "Learning the secret of flight from a bird, was a good deal like learning the secret of magic from a magician." One must be tactful in its application as it applies to verse. "Where the ideas come from, I cannot divulge, and why I continue to do it is primarily for my own amusement."

Mark keeps busy by playing bass guitar in a band (The Fire Apes) and makes for a perfect formula to weave the two obsessions. The band plays original material written, sung, and performed by John Seymour. He also enjoys listening to other live musical talent but is partial to The Fire Apes because of the freedom allowed in the composition of original material. He plays chess on an amateur basis, likes dogs and cats, live oak trees, classic automobiles from the '60s, and his motorcycle. The rest has yet to happen.

www.ingramcontent.com/pod-product-compliance
Lightning Source LLC
Chambersburg PA
CBHW051148120626
46547CB00012B/988